I Am An Awesome Girl

A Collaboration Led by

REGINA "SUNSHINE" ROBINSON

ISBN: 978-1-949266-17-7 Paperback
ISBN: 978-1-949266-18-4 Ebook

DEDICATION

I dedicate this book to the first two girls I loved like they belonged to me…my sisters, Earlisha and Pamelia. They are grown women now, but they were my girls before I was old enough to have my own. My sisters are my heartbeat and my motivations to so much that I do. Their love and support for me is foundational in my life. One thing is for sure, we are tight, and we roll together. My relationship with my sisters is the basis of my love and concern for all of our girls. They taught me how to love other women and in turn, gave me a desire to be a blessing in the lives of our girls. Without them, there is no Regina Sunshine and no Awesome Girls Project.

So today I salute my two best friends in life, a Queen and my Pinky…to the moon and back, it's us til the end.

Regina Sunshine Robinson

TABLE OF CONTENTS

TABLE OF CONTENTS

INTRODUCTION

We all know an Awesome Girl. We see them everywhere we go. We see them singing, running, serving, giving, dancing, inventing, building, loving… just being girls. But although we see them, many don't see themselves. I started the Awesome Girl Awards as a way to celebrate our girls and to let them know that we see them in all their glory and brilliance. And that their uniqueness is a gift to this world.

This book is a celebration of 5 years of the Awesome Girl Project and a beautiful tribute to what makes our girls so awesome. I hope as you read this book that you are inspired…inspired to develop your gifts, inspired to live your dreams, inspired to be who you were created to be.

Remember this….

- ✓ God loves you just the way you are.
- ✓ You are beautiful because you were created in love.
- ✓ You are fearfully and wonderfully made.
- ✓ You have the seeds of greatness within you.
- ✓ You were born to live a victorious life.
- ✓ You are brilliant, gorgeous, talented and fabulous.
- ✓ You are worthy of the best things in life.
- ✓ And one more thing……It's Not Over Til You Win!

CHAPTER 1

MONROE LOVE JOYCE BANKS

Age 6

Why Am I An Awesome Girl?

Being a girl is totally Awesome! We can do anything boys can do; we just look better doing it!

What makes me an awesome girl is that I never give up. I love to read, dance, act, and practice my gymnastics. Sometimes it gets hard learning new things but, I just keep on trying. Learning to read was hard at first but now I love it. Remembering my acting lines and dance moves can be hard too but I keep practicing. Practicing gymnastics is not easy but I love it so

3

much so I will never give up. The reason I never give up is because my mom and dad always tell me to never give up especially when things get hard. They teach me that you only get better when you keep practicing. Since I want to get better at so many things, I'm not going to quit working hard. I have learned to do my best and forget the rest. Saying this makes me feel better because it helps me to focus on just having fun. When I am having fun, I do my best!

Sometimes people ask me what I want to be when I get older and I don't know just yet but whatever I become, I know I will be good at it because I'm going to work hard and that's right, never give up. I admire Beyoncé because she is the best performer I have ever seen. She works really hard and she inspires me to work hard too.

I am thankful for my family because when things get hard, they are there to cheer me up and tell me how proud they are of me. I wish everyone had a family like mine. I love them so much. One day I hope to change the world in my own special way. I want to make people laugh and be happy. When people are happy the world is a better place.

Bio

Monroe Love Joyce Banks is an energetic and smart 6-year-old who enjoys reading, skating, and practicing gymnastics. She is super talented and loves singing dancing and acting. Her dream is to one day be on television inspiring young girls everywhere to love themselves.

CHAPTER 2

SOMMER DAINA BUTLER

Age: 5

Why Am I An Awesome Girl?

I listen to my teacher Ms. Kelley. Sometimes I listen to my parents, well a little bit. I listen to Mommy and Daddy. I Eat my carrots at my mom's house. I eat lots of fruit at Daddy's. I'm Smart. Sometimes I have to tell people what to do. Sometimes I fall but I always get back up. I'm Strong. I can pick up things I'm not big enough to pick up yet. I'm a learner, If I don't know something, I will figure it out.

When I grow up, I want to be a Dentist and a Chef. Because I want to know how to make chicken I like, and I want to make peoples teeth clean. I like to solve math problems; exercise and I love to play with my toys. I also like to go to swim practice. In the future, I just want to do math and not have any bad days.

I admire mommy, daddy and God. They help me with stuff. And they love me. If I could change the world, I would make things right. Some people need to be quiet and do their work so they can get a prize. That's all.

I don't know yet if I want to invent something. You will have to come back to me on that one.

The think I like about being a girl is my hair grows. God made me this way. I don't care what people say about me because this is the way God made me. I'm black and beautiful.

Bio

Sommer Butler is a five year old who's a star student at Georgia Preparatory. When she grows up, she wants to be a Chef and a Dentist. She also wants to swim in the Olympics. Sommer is the daughter of Author and Activist Dainhen Butler.

CHAPTER 3

KANURI ELISE FOWLER -YIKEALO

Age: 7

Why Am I An Awesome Girl?

My name is Kanuri Elise Fowler-Yikealo. I am seven years old and I attend The Children's School of Atlanta. I am very interested in sharing with other people on "Why I believe I'm an Awesome Girl."

In my opinion Awesome means dazzling, amazing, cool, and awesome. As an African American girl, I feel really good and free to do anything I put my mind to.

Some of the most amazing and unique things about me is my ability to be kind. Kindness means being nice to people. For example, not pushing your friends while on the playground, or calling people mean names. I love being kind to my friends and family. For example, a few weeks ago one of my friends did not have lunch one day, and I shared my lunch with her. I believe that "sharing is caring" and it is important in how we treat people every day.

My awesomeness is also shown in the activities I participate in at school or in the community. I attend The Children's School (TCS) of Atlanta. I feel safe and loved at TCS because I feel free to be myself. For example, I am a member of Girl Scouts, Diamond In the Rough, TCS Voices, and Dance Phusion (ballet and tap). I enjoy being a part of the activities and learning new things. These activities have helped me to develop great friendships and have great adult mentors. My teacher, Wilma, died in January of 2019. She was not only my teacher, but a mentor and friend to me for two years. Wilma taught me so many life lessons about myself, and the world around me. Wilma always encouraged me to be my best. She was my hero on earth, and now she is my hero in heaven. I also admire my mom because she is my mom and best friend forever (BFF). Mom gives me cuddles and make me feel safe, loved and cared for and I have a great support of family and friends.

My future dreams include helping homeless people and provide them with food, so they won't be hungry. Also, I am interested in social justice and helping our communities to be fair to all races of people. In order to change the world, I would stop people from fighting, and create peace and harmony. in the world. Lastly, I am interested in inventing a game by using "coding" for all to use. I would name the game Wonderland.

In summary, I am an Awesome girl and I feel special and free about my life. I especially feel free to achieve my dreams, adventure the world, and explore the world as I see it to be.

Words of Encouragement

"You don't have to stay in the dark and hide in the shadows of life. Get out there and be free girl do you what you want and be what you want to be."- Kanuri Elise Fowler-Yikealo

Bio

Kanuri Elise Fowler Yikealo was born on October 25, 2011 in Atlanta, Georgia. Kanuri is the daughter of Dr. Jillian Whatley and Oluyemi Fowler-Yikealo. Kanuri is a second-grade student at The Children's School located in Midtown Atlanta where she is an active member of TCS Voices and Discovery Program. Kanuri recently gave her life to Christ and she attends Voices of Faith where she is actively involved in her Sunday School class. As a young leader, Kanuri is actively involved in Girl Scouts and Diamond in the Rough Youth Development Program where she learns about leadership and community involvement. Kanuri is participating in extracurricular activities, such as, Phusion Dance Company and private art lessons. Kanuri is a budding artist and will showcase her art in the near future. Kanuri has a passion for people and the willingness to help those in need. Kanuri's future is bright!

CHAPTER 4

JANAE' MADISON AKA JJ

Age: 7

Why Am I An Awesome Girl?

JANAE is seven years old AND MOMMIES Little Glamour Girl! Janae' is full of PASSION & PERSONALITY which makes her an awesome Girl. She truly is all about "mommy and me" Fitness inspiring daughters and moms to take a "time-out" for fitness. She is awesome because she has a genuine heart for helping people. Janae' is determined and very focus for her age.

The words that describe her are:

Awesome, Exciting, Humble Responsible and Friendly.

Her promise is to be The Best she can be letting her light shine for the world to see. She pledges to be nice, kind, and respectful everywhere she goes. Demonstrate courage and motivate and inspire young girls to believe in themselves.

Jane wants to be a dance fitness instructor, teacher and cosmetologist

Janae' likes to workout, dance play the piano, and do gymnastics.

Janae' says she admires her mommy because she is "my biggest cheerleader. She shows me how to be confident & brave and never give up!!

Janae's dreams for the future is to live a long healthy life. Believe in whatever I can do. Have a Dance Fitness Studio.

Janae said to change the world she would tell people to always be nice and treat people well, be humble, and inspiring.

Janae' said she would invent an effort machine to put effort in everything you do.

Janae' likes being a girl because you can dress up pretty and show a lot of style and personality.

Bio

Janae' is 7 years old and mommies' Little Glamour Girl! Janae' is full of PASSION & PERSONALITY which makes her an Awesome Girl!! Janae is all about "Mommy & Me" Fitness which is a signature program she does working out with her mom motivating moms and their children to work out together. Janae has a genuine heart for helping people. Janae' is determined and very focus for her age. She is truly an awesome little Girl and it shows in her personality. When you watch her videos, she is sure to capture your heart. Because, this Little Glamour Girl is "ALL HEART".

CHAPTER 5

ZIGGY AND TOOTIE QUINN

Ages: Ziggy 9 and Tootie 7

Why Are We Awesome Girls?

We are Ziggy and Tootie, founders and CEOs of Ziggy and Tootie Cakes! And we are awesome girls because we have amazing parents!

Both of our parents served in the United States Air Force for over 20 years; and we were born on Lakenheath Royal Air Base in England. Although our parents divorced shortly after we were born, they vowed to make us their number one priority. Our parents refused to allow us to become a statistic. Our dad bought a house ten minutes away from our mom and we get to hang out at his house all the time! Our dad takes us to all our softball and soccer practices and games. He even coaches sometimes too. We often go to Mississippi with our dad and it is there where he teaches us how to hunt and fish. When were two and three years old, our dad bought us rental property; making us kid real estate investors.

Our mom is amazing too! She never lets anything get in our way of being successful. In 2012 she left her second career as a schoolteacher to homeschool us. In homeschooling us, she not only taught us how to read and write and do math, bust she also taught us how to CODE and start a business from scratch. In 2014 we launched our first business, Ziggy and Tootie Cakes from our mom's kitchen table. Because we were doing so well in business, at the ages of three and four, our mom enrolled us into The Black Business School with Dr. Boyce Watkins. In business school we learned how to set and reach our business goals. In January 2019, with help from our mom, we achieved our goal of owning a bakery; making us the youngest retail bakery owners in the United States.

We are awesome girls because we believe in giving just as much as we receive. In May 2019 we started our nonprofit foundation so that we can partner with other organizations and serve our community on a larger scale. Through our foundation we teach entrepreneurship and STEM to other kids in our community. We volunteer and speak at schools and youth centers on the topic of Baking Up A Business! We also host live interactive STEM workshops on the integration of science, math, technology, design and engineering of baking.

We could not be the awesome girls that we are without loving and supportive parents like our mom and dad. As kid real estate investors and entrepreneurs, we rely on our mom and dad to provide us with a solid education, to manager our business affairs and to juggle our busy schedule and they do an amazing job!

Words of Encouragement

When you give, your hand is open to receive. Give just as much as you expect to receive in life.

Affirmations, and words they live by:

1. I was born to lead!

2. I am black, gifted and talented!

3. I am amazing!

4. The more I give the more I receive.

5. God will always place me in the presence of great people.

Bio

Ziggy and Tootie are two young cake moguls that are mastering the art of kid-entrepreneurship in the 21st century! In Jan 2019, they opened their very own bakery, making them the youngest retail bakery owners in the world! Through their earning, they have funded 3 first-class vacations to Disney World and to Great Wolf Lodge. These two cake moguls have also won over $7K in pitch competitions. Ziggy and Tootie are not only cake designers, but they are also award-winning authors, educators and public speakers.

CHAPTER 6

MCKINZIE BAKER

Age: 8

Why Am I An Awesome Girl?

My name is McKinzie, I am eight years old and I am sooooo awesome!

Why am I awesome you might ask? Because God says so.

I am also awesome because I like to do lots of things like painting pictures on canvases, playing basketball, making jewelry like chokers, bracelets and necklaces made from beads, rubber bands and paper clips. I also enjoy playing with my friends, being

17

with my family and love them with all my heart. I like to do things like help mommy with her events, I love drawing, celebrating my birthday, Easter and Christmas. I am also awesome because I am stylish and fashionable like the model Naomi Campbell; I am a superstar!

I am also awesome because I am smart, pretty, and I love to help people. I like taking care of others, making new friends and playing with my old friends named Azaria, Kaitlin, Patrick, and Aubrey who have different skin colors and from many nationalities. I am awesome because I am comfortable in my brown skin and like to encourage other little girls to be just as comfortable and confident in their skin no matter what color it is.

I am awesome because I am great in gymnastics and doing bridge. I am awesome because when I look in the mirror, I know that I am beautiful. I am awesome because I have a beautiful voice and love to sing.

I am awesome because I am creative and like to dress up in pretty dresses and put on jewels and twirl and twirl until I am dizzy. I am awesome because I believe in sharing and laughing at the silliest things, running and practicing cartwheels and riding my bicycle.

I am awesome because when I was five, I walked with my mommy and many others to bring awareness to domestic violence and people that have been hurt by it. I am awesome because each year, I help the homeless and misfortunate people by blessing them with pictures, smiles, and hugs to show that I care.

I am awesome because my black is beautiful. I am awesome because I like to watch Ariana Grande, Sia, Beyoncé, JoJo Siwa, and Dua Lipa and sing along with their lyrics, they make feel super happy because they are fancy just like me. I am awesome because I love to imagine that one day, I will be a singer like Ariana Grande, an artist and paint and draw and make money, and be a model and travel around the world and makes wherever I go or bring my friends with me when I travel.

I am awesome because I like to break boundaries and do different things that takes be outside of a box, pushing me to be unique and exciting while being smart in school and exploring the possibilities that surround me.

McKinzie Baker's Affirmation

I am beautiful just the way I am.

Bio

McKinzie Alise Baker was born in Johns Creek, Georgia and is currently a resident of Lawrenceville, Georgia where she resides with her mommy. McKinzie is eight-years old, in the second grade, a member of the Shooting Stars gymnastics team, a humanitarian by inheritance, and a Spark and Ring Runner in the Awana Bible Study Program. McKinzie also helps her mother through coordinate and manage the Girls of Virtue Empowered Program where she helps set-up and share her vision of what a G.O.V.E. looks at feels like to girls between the ages of 6- years old. She plans to become an artist, model, and singer when she graduates from high school while continuing her volunteer work in the community.

CHAPTER 7

OLIVIA ELIZABETH STANLEY

Age: 8

Why Am I An Awesome Girl?

Strong, beautiful, loyal, determine, all words that describe an awesome girl. These words describe me. I am an awesome girl. I am strong. I encourage my friends at school. I remind them of God's love for them. I am beautiful. I love my brown skin and my curly hair. I am perfect just the way God made me. I am determined. Giving up is not an option. I am loyal to my faith and my family. I will never wonder away from my faith and what I believe. I love my family. I serve and donate both my time and resources. My family and I

21

collect pop tabs to give to the Ronald McDonald house to pay for the room and board of families with sick children while their loved ones are in the hospital. I also participate in Operation Christmas. Each year I pick a boy or girl to gift a Christmas box. The goal is to make sure no child has no gifts on Christmas morning. I am Legendary! My hero is my father. He loves me with all his heart. I think he is courageous. He works hard to take care of me, mom, and Cuddles. When I grow up, I would like to be a clothing designer. If I could make something that would change people's lives it would be a robot that walks pets. Lots of families travel and work hard. The robot would help them make sure their pets are taken care of. Some of my favorite things to do are draw and read. I also enjoy playing with my Bunny Cuddles. Someone I admire is my mom. She always takes care of me and dad even when she is tired or does not feel well. She is loyal, joyful, and kind. She always tells me I can do anything, and I believe her!

Affirmations

I am beautiful just the way I am.

Never be Afraid God is With You!

I trust God!

I have Faith in God!

I Expect God!

Bio

Olivia Elizabeth Stanley was born in Cary, NC on March 25, 2011. She is the daughter of Oliver & Pamelia Stanley. Olivia loves to sing, sew, draw, and read. She attends Grace Christian School in Raleigh, NC. She is a published author and illustrator. She is also a designer of doll clothing and accessories. Her goal when she grows up is to be Legendary!

CHAPTER 8

DE'ZYRE WILLIAMS

Age: 8

Why Am I An Awesome Girl?

All people are awesome in many ways. Being awesome can be conveyed as exploring talents, helping others, being positive, and being prosocial. However, an awesome girl is an elite young woman that is confident and empowers others. This chapter aims to describe why girls are awesome, why I believe that I am an awesome girl, and to empower other girls to be awesome.

To begin with, girls are awesome because girls can do anything they want if they try. There are so many girls all over the world that are awesome, and they are so encouraging by doing anything they want to do. There are so many people that are not proud of us girls for doing the things that we believe. However, we as girls have to encourage other girls that they can do anything if they believe they can. We also have to teach other girls that having supporters is very important to help us along the way. Girls have many different talents that they can do. Girls can sing, dance, write books, and many other gifts and talents. All girls have talents or gifts, but they have to believe that they can conquer everything in order to be awesome.

Moreover, I am awesome because I can encourage others to do what they believe. I am also awesome because I have my own business and my own books that I authored. I can teach others how to make friends and other social skills with my books. I am talented. I am a blue belt in mixed martial arts and a gymnast. I help others that are in need of help and I give people advice.

Conclusively, I want to encourage you to remember five affirmations for being awesome, One, I am an attraction of everything that I De'Zyre (desire). Two, I express my de'zyres (desire) through my passion. Three, I am all that I de'zyre (desire) to be for the greatness of myself and others. Four, I am confident and powerful. Lastly, "If you can dream it, you can do it" by Walt Disney.

Bio

De'Zyre (pronounced Desire) Williams is an 8-year-old Author, Inspirational Speaker, Actress, & CEO/Owner of De'Zyre Williams Enterprises, LLC. De'Zyre is from Plymouth, North Carolina. She enjoys writing, reading, Martial Arts, Gymnastics, traveling, and spending time with her family. Contact De'Zyre at www.dezyrewilliamsenterprises.com

CHAPTER 9

MILAN WALLER

Age: 9

Why I Believe I Am An Awesome Girl

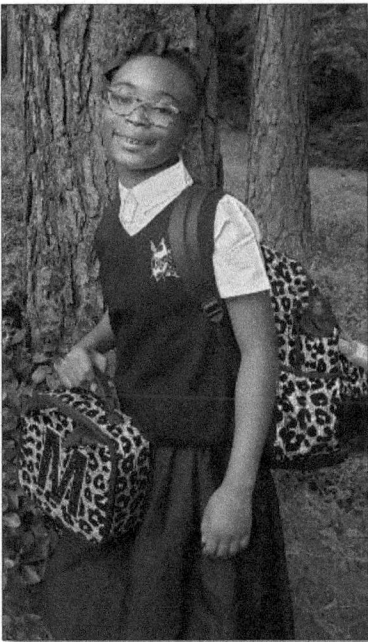

Milan believes she is an awesome girl, because she plans, prepares, and executes her dreams and goals. Milan's heart leads her, but her faith in Good guides her. She believes it's important to think about goals that will impact and help others, as well as, herself. Her dream is to become a Bio-Medical Engineer and later attain her "M.D.". Milan desires to develop her own line assistive medical technology.

As a civic thought leader, Milan has been recognized by the Girl Scouts

25

of America as a young entrepreneur for her outstanding cookie sales and devotion to her faith. From kindergarten to third grade, Milan was recognized by Victory World Christian School for her volunteerism and civic leadership with the Junior League of Atlanta. The Junior League of Atlanta – an exclusively educational and charitable organization of women committed to promoting volunteerism, developing the potential of women, and improving the community through the action and leadership of trained volunteers. Milan served as a Little Black Dress Advocate with the Junior League of Atlanta and Victory World Christian School made a charitable contribution to the JLA on her behalf. While participating in this initiative to raise financial donations and awareness on the impact of generational poverty on families in Metro-Atlanta, Milan shared her personal testimony with hundreds of children of how she and her mother overcame situational poverty.

In addition to this work, Milan has been deeply committed and involved in the advancement of STEM work and innovations for girls. She also serves her community by actively serving as an active member of the Stone Mountain Chapter of Jack and Jill of America, Incorporated, Junior Girl Scouts of America, Greater Atlanta Chapter, and an active member of the Victory World School Robotics team. Her interests include any STEM activities, entrepreneurship, learning about the stock market, reading novels, riding horses at Ellenwood Equestrian Center, and playing the piano at Piano Keys for Christ.

Milan strives to utilize every available platform in her efforts to raise awareness about medical issues affecting students with invisible disabilities, such as allergies, asthma, and eczema. She has presented at tech workshops and most recently assisted with facilitating a discussion at a Square workshop on "Tiktok". Milan will launch her business and not-for-profit organization in December of 2019.

As committed as she is to the City of Atlanta, she is also devoted to raising awareness of the longstanding impact of the "Flint Water

Crisis". She enjoys visiting her family in Flint, Michigan and serving at Pentecostal Outreach with her grandmother. She is a proud member of Victory World Church in Norcross, Georgia. Milan's personal strengths are as impressive as her intellectual accomplishments.

Affirmations

I love myself, I believe in myself, and I am genius! What is a leader? A leader is an independent that operates with integrity. What is integrity? Doing the right thing, when no one is watching. I trust in the Lord with all my heart and lean not unto my own understanding. In all my ways I acknowledge HIM, and HE directs my path.

Bio

Miss Milan Waller, an innovator, civic leader, and young trailblazer hails from Atlanta, Georgia. She is the beloved daughter of Ms. Melissa Waller and granddaughter of Dr. Steven and Roberta Waller. Milan is a budding and bright fourth grader at The Wilson Academy in Lithonia, Georgia. She continually displays respect, compassion, and gratitude for those whom and with whom she serves, her community, her friends, and most of all her family.

CHAPTER 10

ZAYDAH LOTALLAH

Age: 10

Why Am I An Awesome Girl?

I am an awesome girl because I overcome my challenges and work hard towards my dreams.

One of the challenges I was faced with was bullying, and at the time I felt completely alone. When I would go to school a lot of the children would make fun of me because I wouldn't act like them or hang around with them. I know you guys are like, "Wait, why didn't you hang out with them, and why were you not like them?" Well,

I would have liked to hang out with them, and I did try to, but they were never nice to me or anyone else. I felt like they didn't like me because I was really different from everyone in my classroom. I always listened to the teacher and worked very hard. They never listened to the teacher and were constantly playing when it was time to work. However, by the end of the first semester they had almost the whole class bullying each other, and the teacher didn't do anything about it.

The teacher I had was blindsided when it came to bullying and being treated unfairly, so she eventually ended up with a whole classroom of bullies. I knew that I shouldn't be associating with these kids, but my teacher would get mad when I said that I wanted to avoid interacting with them. In my head I asked, "If the other kids were bullies and being disrespectful, why would anyone want me to be like them?"

One day we got to eat outside. It was a hot day, but two students and I were sitting in the sun. We had gotten our lunch first, so we got to choose where we sat. As the other kids came in, they all sat in the shade. After a little while, the other two kids who were sitting with me left to sit in the shade. I was the only person left sitting in the sun because I liked it, and I don't follow what everyone else does. Then out of the blue my teacher yells, "This is why nobody likes you!" It caught me completely of guard! She told me that I should go sit over there with her and everyone else. To stop her from saying something else hurtful, I did what she said. In that moment I felt like she did not even like me at all. But you know what? I realized that she was not a good role model for me either. So, I decided that it does not matter what anyone else thinks. I am who I am, and I am not going to change.

The rest of the year I worked hard and tried to stay true to myself. One of my dreams is to get all A's and go to Harvard. I worked toward my dream for that year and I got all A's.

For all of you girls out there who are being treated unfairly I am here for you. If you stay true to YOU, you can accomplish anything.

Affirmations

1. I attract good people into my life.

2. I have people who love me even in hard times.

3. I am getting closer to my dreams every day.

4. I am beautiful and unique just the way I am.

5. I love myself and do the best I can every day.

Bio:

Zaydah Lotallah is a speaker, actress, singer and author all while maintaining excellent grades in elementary school. She most recently starred as Annie in her school play and delivered a speech at a TedX Youth event. Zaydah hopes to use these public skills and platforms to make the world a better place, especially in the areas of social justice and civil rights. Her greatest dream is to be President of the United States, so that she may have the greatest impact. While not at the White House yet, she lives just outside of Atlanta, GA with her parents and two younger brothers.

CHAPTER 11

JANAE KANU

Age: 11

Why Am I An Awesome Girl?

Hey there gorgeous! Do you know that you're awesome? Well if you don't, you may feel differently after this chapter. My name is Janae Kanu and I am going to tell you why I am an awesome girl, and why you are awesome too!

My name is Janae Kanu. I am eleven years old and in the sixth grade. I live in Georgia. I'm a straight A student and the oldest of five- which consist of three sisters, one brother, and me. I have a big and loving family. Especially my mom, grandma, dad, aunt, and one of my sisters, Jaela. I love them so much!

I am an awesome girl because I am free to be myself, with all my craziness and flaws, and I NEVER give up. Most importantly I am an actress/model that will help create social change. I have a big heart for helping people. I have a big passion for helping people and I want to donate money as well as cook homemade meals and give it to people in need. This way people can never go hungry. If people ever ask me "Janae, how do you it?" I'll just say, "It's the God in me."

I want to be the inspiration that you see on TV I want everyone to see the light that is inside of me. I am an actress and model because I want to prove to girls like you that if I can do this, then you can do anything that you put your mind to. No matter what anyone tells you.

I'm not the only person that is awesome though, you are awesome too! Whether you're short, tall, or you have pimples, big feet, or even small feet you are beautiful and perfect just the way you are. God made you that way and you are awesome. And no matter what age (5,6, or even 57) YOU can make a difference. So how will you use your awesomeness to change the world?

Affirmations

Say these words to confirm your awesomeness:

- I am pretty

- I am smart

- I am funny

- I can accomplish anything

- I will change the world for the better

- I will make a difference

- I will make my mark in the world

- Nothing and no one can stop me

- I am fierce and fearless

- I am loved

- I am an awesome girl

Thank you

- Ms. Regina Sunshine

-Ms. Karana

- Ms. Angela

-The support from my family and friends

You're pretty cool!

I love who you are and everything you are going to be.

Until next time,

Janae Kanu

Bio

Janae Kanu is a beautiful girl with a big heart and a bright spirit that genuinely cares about making the world a better place. A natural and talented child actress and model, Janae has immense skills with abilities to play comedic and dramatic roles. From a small age, Janae has desired to bring a loving and positive presence to the entertainment industry, as well as help others in need to create the positive change within society. Pursuing her passion, Janae entered to compete at the National Discovery Spotlight Showcase in Charleston, SC for acting and modeling and became a finalist at her first competition! A perpetual honor roll student, Janae has been the lead in school plays, attended peer leadership conferences, modeled on runway shows, and even became Vice President of her school 2 years ago. Janae is well on her way to achieving her dream to becoming a positive leading for the entertainment industry.

CHAPTER 12

JACEY CUFFIE

Age: 13

Why Am I An Awesome Girl?

What makes a person awesome? Everybody on this Earth has different qualities that make them great and unique. The word awesome makes me awesome. 'A' is for Ambitious. Whatever I do in life, whether it is walking my dog or writing a book report, I plan to be successful. I am open to change and have high expectations for myself. 'W' is for Worthy. I am an important human being in this world and know I am worthy enough to change it. All of us are worthy enough to change it. The first 'E' is for Empowering. I want everyone to know that they should be confident in who they are and be the best person they can possibly be. Being comfortable in your own skin is very important. 'S' is for smart. I have very good grades in school and have received many academic awards. In addition, I am smart enough to make wise decisions which will affect me in the future. 'O' is for optimistic. I always try to look on the bright side of things. While some people may think of the glass half empty, I will always see the glass half full. 'M' is for magnificent. I am an admirable person on this Earth, and I do inspiring things. I am a natural born leader and people look up to me. Lastly, 'E' is for Enough.

I know that I do not have to change for any person on this earth. Who I truly am will always be enough. I know that I am a daughter of God, and He made me the exact way He wants me to be. In my journey of life, I have learned these things: I can accomplish anything I put my mind to. Nothing or no one will get in the way of my dreams and aspirations. I believe in myself and I have great confidence in my abilities. Although I am not perfect, I will not change who I am to conform to someone else. I love and approve of myself. I know that who I am is great and that I love being me. I am somebody special. I know that I am somebody. I can do this. Lastly, I have the power to change the world. I am a believer that I will change this world for the better and change the lives of people living on this lavish planet. I am awesome and so are you.

Bio

Hello! My name is Jacey Cuffie. I enjoy reading and writing. I am a competition dancer and cheer for the eighth-grade football team. I am in a club at my school called, "Destiny Daughters of Promise," a leadership program, converting girls into powerful young women. I am not sure what I want to be when I grow up; however, I will always remember, "The future depends on what you do today."- Gandhi.

CHAPTER 13

ZOE GORE

Age: 15

Why Am I An Awesome Girl?

Why do I believe I'm an Awesome? I believe that I'm an Awesome girl because I am strong. This means this that I am capable of doing whatever I put my mind to. I have strong goals that I want to accomplish in life. I also believe that I'm an awesome girl because I believe in myself. I have to believe in myself to have a good mindset. This means that I have to have confidence in myself to put in the effort that I'm getting out. The other reason that I believe that I am an awesome girl is that I don't care what any haters have to say about me because if I am happy in myself and in Jesus. I also believe that I am an awesome girl is because I can reach my standers in my life. I believe that I'm an awesome girl because I encourage people to try at best and don't give up. I also believe that I am an awesome girl because I have talents that I love to use no matter what comes my way I will always the talents that Jesus gave me. I also believe that I an awesome girl because I believe in Jesus Christ because without him, I will be nothing in life I wouldn't be able to do the things that I do if it wasn't for him. I believe that I am an awesome girl because I help my elders the most important elders that I will respect is my Mother she is my rock I love her every day in my life she inspires me every day so to my Mother Mrs. Geraldine Gore I love you and Thank you for playing a big role in my life. This is the Affirmation that encourages me, and I believe it will encourage other girls. It is a bible verse 1Corinthians 10:13 And it says, "No temptation has overtaken you except what is common to mankind." And God is faithful; he will not let you be tempted beyond what you can bear. But when you are tempted, he will also provide a way out so that you can endure it. It means to me that no matter what you are going through God will always see you through no temptations can get through you when you are with God.

Encouragement

1. The first thing that encourages me to keep me going is Jesus. I have to keep looking towards Him for everything that I go through.

2. The second thing that keeps me going is my Mother Geraldine Gore. She always tells me that I can do something even though it gets hard. She always keeps a positive attitude that keeps me going.

3. The third thing that keeps me going is myself. I have to keep a

positive attitude towards myself and others.

4. The Fourth that keeps me going is my friend. She talks to me every day and sends positive quotes that keeps me going.

5. The Final thing that keeps me going is singing. I love to sing, and it keeps my mood happy and smiling.

Bio

Zoe Patsy Gore is the daughter of Thomas Earl and Geraldine Gore and is the youngest of 5 girls. She is a ninth grader at South Columbus High School in Tabor City, NC and attends Mitchell Sea Missionary Baptist Church in Green Sea, SC. Zoe enjoys singing in the church choir, being a part of the praise and worship team and dancing on the church praise team. Zoe also enjoys working with the youth at Finklea Community Center. She plans to attend North Carolina A& T State University to pursue a career as a Psychologist.

CHAPTER 14

ASHALAH MICHELLE

Age: 15

Why Am I An Awesome Girl?

I am an awesome girl because that all people are awesome in their own way. For me, awesomeness starts on the inside. I am very caring. I am confident. I am intelligent.

I am very ambitious! I started my entrepreneurial journey at age 9 when I first discovered my passion for baking. I started to watch YouTube videos to practice my craft. At age 12 I finally started my business Cook Me Up A Notch where I cater cookies, cakes, and culinary creations.

I love my family!!! I am awesome because I have the best support system in the world!! My mother and brother are the best in the world. At first my mother didn't think that I wasn't passionate about baking, so I had to prove that I really wanted to bake. Once I did that my mother hooked on like a like a fish finding a worm on a hook. Pushing me to following my dreams and to step outside my comfort zone. My brother is just along for the ride helping the best way he can.

I am an awesome girl because I am compassionate. I love to give back with my family as we feed the homeless with my mother's non-profit Greater Giving. Last Christmas my family and I worked with another non-profit to get back by getting people in need care packages that included undergarments, clothes, food kits, and drinks. We went under the bridges in Atlanta and handed these care packages out and we even prayed for them too. My family and I try to give back all year round by its our favorite time to give back are the holidays. The holidays really do bring people together!!!

I am an awesome girl because I am inspiring. I know that I am inspiring because many people have told me that I inspired them to start their own business. My brother even says that inspire him and that is way he started his own t-shirt company!

To be an awesome girl is to be awesome with an amazing personally. To be the best you, you can be. To never change who you are for anyone. To believe in yourself and your dreams. If I can be an awesome girl, you can be too!

*WHAT HAVE YOU OVERCOME INTERNALLY AND EXTERNALLY?:

The one thing that has been an ongoing thing that I've had to overcome internally was my self-worth. Many times I didn't know what I deserved and afraid to truly go after what I wanted. I thank God for a mother that pushed me until my confidence in myself grew. Yet, with every level there is still things that make me say to myself, "Do I deserve this and if so, can you do this?" I think this lack of self-worth or confidence stemmed from my absence of a father and just the realness surrounding my birth. It is a hard topic for me to discuss and one day I will share it with the world. Just know that sometimes you wonder why did God place you here on this Earth in that way. My mom always told me the day she found out she was pregnant she asked God the same question I asked and he replied, "She will be a gift to this world. She will never go without!" At first I thought she was just saying that to make me feel good but when I was about 9 or 10 years old, I wrote a note to go in my prayer closet or "War Room" and I asked him to show me my purpose. I didn't know that was what he was doing as I experienced baking with my grandma. Everything seemed so magical. As I touched the flour, the sound of pouring the milk, creating and forming the biscuits with my hands, and even my grandma's voice as she talked me through the steps. This was my purpose! Its like my heart was in it, my mind could see it, and I felt all joyful inside about it. I begged my mom for 2 years before she was able to see the glow in me. She said that one day God spoke to her just as he did when she was pregnant and said, "This is the gift!" She has helped me live my dream ever since.

So, through it all, since we've officially started my business Cook Me Up A Notch in 2016, she has been there helping me to build and live it. God has taught us many hard lessons and we've seen some amazing victories. We've lived through homelessness, lost of friends and family, my grandma passing away, bad business deals, and going completely broke. Yet we've persevered due to our faith in God, focus on mental health and therapeutic practices, continuous training and development both personally and in business, staying true to our set family times, and loving one another. My mom has always raised my brother and I alone with lack of support or family. I've learned from her how to lean on God and this I believe is what really makes me an awesome girl!

To be an awesome girl is to be the best you God has made you to be. I am walking in my purpose with God leading the way and this is the only best me I know how to be!

Bio

Ashalah Michelle Wright is a teen business owner, honor student, 4x Author, S.T.E.A.M. advocate, and pastry chef. Heading toward her "Sweet 16", the Pastry Princess of Atlanta has made a yummy sweet name for herself, as she shares her story and craft with children all over the world. She believes that every girl and boy have an awesome gift and with models and mentors like her, they can be guided in the right way. Her new program, Bakeology 101: A Guide to Baking With S.T.E.A.M demonstrates her skills as an expert and her beliefs that with hard work, dreams can come true! Learn more about Chef Ashalah Michelle at www.cookmeupanotch.com

CHAPTER 15

LAURYN STRONG

Age: 17

Why Am I An Awesome Girl?

Often times I ask myself "How did I become this awesome girl that inspires so many young people and adults to strive for their goals?" I work hard for what I believe in, I don't give up, I am very empathetic, and I am very confident in the things I do and for that I am an awesome girl! Ever since I was a little girl, I have been in the kitchen helping my family cook home cooked meals and baked goods. Growing up it was my mom, my dad, and my two brothers always home cooking different types of meals such as Blue corn meal fried chicken, Smoked apple sausage with curry lentils and much more. Being the only girl in the house, everyone expected more from me, so I knew I needed to always try to do my best in everything I do and watch how I carried myself. Now being a big sister of three girls I am more mindful of how I speak and act to others because I know they look up to me and is watching how I carry myself as well. Ever since I was a little girl I was taught how to hustle, grind and be genuine. My dad always said, "To hustle you must always move forward to achieve your goals and do it with a sense of urgency."

It became really easy to put more of my time and attention into my craft, hobbies, school, and social life that I never sought out balance. I got off track with God. I let those little temptations and that drive to always move forward that I forgot to stop and thank him for blessing me with my talent. I got so distracted that I got off track with my faith practices and didn't dedicate a little one on one time with God each day. In 1st grade my grandmother would pick me up every day from school and we would take a trip to "John's" mini market down the street. We would buy ingredients needed to recreate Rachael Ray meals that we learned from watching her afternoon segment. Every day I grew to love cooking with my grandmother because I enjoyed learning new techniques and trying them out. When I was eight years old, I baked my first cake with my dad for my mother's birthday and ever since then I had this passion for baking. Throughout the years I focused on perfecting my craft so I can become well known for having the best cupcakes in Atlanta.

Being a teenager, maintaining all A' and B's, and running a catering business can be very time consuming but it is all worth it if your passionate about it. A lot of upcoming entrepreneurs can lose sight that you must work hard for what you want, especially when there are many people trying to perfect the same craft as you. When you are focused on always being better than your competition then you are not focusing on what's best for your business. Every day you should be trying to compete with the person you were yesterday, learning and growing from your mistakes. Never beat yourself up for what may seem like a mistake. You must know that it was necessary for you to walk that path to learn those lessons.

Some words that I think describe me are passionate, hardworking, and perfectionist. I think I am passionate because I really love what I do, and I like seeing people react to the food that I made. It is just something about baking and creating creative meals and desserts that no one ever thinks of. I am hardworking because I sacrifice a lot to be the person I am today and work hard to serve my family and community.

I am on the varsity volleyball team which I spend hours training to not only be the best for myself but for my team. I am always studying and putting effort to be involved in school to maintain good grades and one day be able to go to whatever school I desire. Some nights I stay up late just to get homework, study for a test, finish cupcake orders, or prepare for my events. I sacrifice a lot of social time to work on my business, school, and volleyball that it becomes a little challenging to hang out with my friends. Even though it becomes challenging I still always make time to hang out with the people I love, and I know no matter what my family and friends have my back and is there to support me in anything I do.

I am an awesome girl not only because I work hard but it is because I have a strong support system to help guide me and other amazing young girls supporting me as well. I am a warrior and warriors do not give up!

Bio

Chef Lala is a 17-year-old entrepreneur that has her own catering company known as Lala's Sugar & Spice. She has been baking since she was 6 years old and started her company in 2016. She was introduced in the food industry by her mentor Tregaye Frazier who is Food Network Star season 12 winner and winner of Guy's Grocery Games. She was the 2017 Junior Atlanta's Trailblazer Award's recipient. Lala loves making creative cupcakes that bring flavor and life to the pallet such as her delicious Maple Bourbon Cupcakes, Chicken and waffles Cupcakes; Berry, Chocolate Oreo, Strawberry filled Cupcakes and much more. She has won multiple junior competitions and has been a vendor at the Atlanta Ice Cream Festival for three years in a row. Chef Lala has also been honored to help provide service in the Chef of the Worlds event for two years in a row.

CHAPTER 16

JASMINE WITT

Age: 17

Why Am I An Awesome Girl?

History gives us countless examples of amazing women who used their talents to change the world for the better. At first, they were forced to do it in the background, hiding behind fake names or husbands and fathers with power. Many of them never received credit for their achievements. Nefertiti, an ancient Egyptian Queen, is believed to have changed her name and ruled as "king" of Egypt after her husband died.

51

She was forgotten until archaeologists stumbled upon a portrait of her, and now she is regarded as one of the most beautiful women from the ancient world. Rosalind Franklin, an American scientist, discovered the structure of a DNA molecule, only to have the credit stolen by her associates, simply because she was female. Other women, however, are forever remembered for their successes. When Amelia Earhart was only 24 years old, she became the first female to fly alone; 122 years later, Earhart remains a role model for young girls everywhere. Commemorated as one of the most influential females in the movement for women's suffrage, Susan B. Anthony cast a vote for her voice and for all those like hers.

These examples don't even begin to scratch the surface of the myriad women that have transformed society, and you have the ability to do it too. You don't have to change the whole world to be great. It takes more than one person to make a difference, and there are plenty of things that make you every bit as special as these women. Maybe it's the way your smile has the ability to brighten up someone's whole day. Maybe it's how you can understand math equations without even thinking about them. Maybe you can write poems that are so beautiful they move people to tears. Or maybe it's simply the way you love the people around you. Whatever it is, it makes you the person that you were made to be. God aligned the whole universe so you could be born just the way you are, so you must be pretty darn important. And that's amazing.

Fair warning: the world will try to belittle you. Tell you that pretty is all you will ever be… that you can't reach your dreams and are bound to serve people of higher stature than you for the rest of your life. I want you to know that they are wrong. You have the power to do anything you put your mind to. You have the ability to change the rules and the world, to make a difference. Use that power. Leave the world a better place than you found it. Make it better for the awesome girls that surround you now, and those that will surely come after you. Make it easier for them to achieve their goals so that they can reach even higher bounds. And, make sure you always remember just how much you really are worth. Never let anyone treat you like less than the queen you are. Because you are a queen. And so am I. We are all awesome girls destined for even more awesome things.

So, rule the kingdom of your life as Nefertiti did. Make world-changing discoveries like Rosalind. Adopt Amelia's bravery. Use your voice to speak for those that don't have one, like Susan did. Whatever you do, do it like the amazing girl you are.

Affirmations

You don't have to be perfect; you just have to try.

The God who made mountains, oceans, and galaxies made you too.

Your love is worth more than you could ever imagine.

You were born with everything you need inside of you.

The world is your oyster.

Bio

Jasmine Witt is a seventeen-year-old girl who loves books, coffee, and Jesus. Her mission in life is to travel as many places as she can and love everyone she meets along the way. Born and raised in a small town in South Carolina, Jasmine knows there's nothing quite as good as a big glass of sweet tea in the company of good people. She believes that there's nothing a nice bubble bath can't fix, and that our main purpose on Earth is to spread as much love and kindness as we can, and what better place to start than building up the amazing girls around you?

CHAPTER 17

CAMILLE BROWN

Age: 18

Why Am I An Awesome Girl?

My name is Camille Brown and I believe that I'm an awesome girl because I have utilized my crafts and talents in order to raise awareness of numerous topics and usher my audience into happiness.

I recently graduated high school with a 3.95 GPA and received an array of recognitions throughout my four years. Some of these honors included receiving an award for graduating top of my class, being praised for maintaining good behavior, and having a good relationship with my teachers.

Although on paper my high school life appeared to be perfect, socially I suffered greatly during my first two years. In fact, during my freshman and sophomore years, I was bullied by different groups of people due to possessing unique views, interests, and hobbies. This resulted in self-doubt, lack of confidence, and self-rejection. Often times victims of bullying are told to "get over" the pain and that their emotional turmoil will disappear once the emotional abuse stops. However, I am living proof that the roots of bullying run deep and have the potential to affect individuals several years later. Consequently, I promised myself that I would remain strong and fight the negative thoughts in order to use my experiences to help someone else. In fact, during my junior and senior years I broke outside of my shell by giving advice to several individuals and raising awareness of the topic at my county's school system meeting.

In addition to being an anti-bullying advocate, I possess an exceptional musical talent. In fact, my parents told me I wrote my first song at age one and began my classical music journey at the age of four. Ever since then, God has blessed with the privilege to have played before hundreds of people at music festivals, private events, and to have played alongside award-winning musicians. However, my greatest joy comes from hearing how God has utilized my gifts and talents in order to change someone else's life.

A few years ago, I played at a fundraiser for a terminally ill child who was initially not expected to live. Even though at the time I did not understand the full context of his illness, I was determined to open my ears to the sweet notes of heaven in order to allow God to reverse the boy's condition. I knew this was true when as soon as I started playing, the young boy's eyes lit up with life. After the fundraiser, I waited anxiously for weeks to hear of the child's status. You can only imagine the happiness I felt when I learned that he not only recovered from the treatment but also reached a state of remission! From that moment

I realized just how powerful my efforts towards helping others can be. Consequently, I promised myself that I would dedicate the rest of my life towards helping others. Whether I raise awareness against bullying, inspire girls around the world, or aid the afflicted, my purpose is tied into being a healer.

Affirmation: "Love yourself first because that's who you'll be spending the rest of your life with."—unknown

Bio

Violinist Camille wrote her first song at age one, enjoys teaching herself numerous instruments, and producing her musical ideas. Additionally, Camille is classically trained, can play anything by ear and has offered her services at: weddings, music festivals, Christmas parties, and other events. You can reach her at FlowerViolinist@Hotmail.com, follow her on Twitter @TheFlower02, and can subscribe to her YouTube channel: TheFlower02.

CHAPTER 18

JAYEL PRIESTER

Age: 18

Why Am I An Awesome Girl

The thing I love the most about being a girl is surprising people with what I'm capable of. To the outside world I look like a regular teenage girl…but when they learn I am a young entrepreneur with nothing but ambition and a big future it's the best feeling in the world.

My name is Jayel Priester and I am the Owner and Lead Designer of Kuponya. I am outgoing, passionate, ambitious, and creative. My favorite part about being a young entrepreneur is the fact I get to have fun on both side of business and personal life!

During my free time my favorite things to do are play video games, roller skate and spend time with my family. While during business hours my favorite thing to do is taking an idea and making it a reality.

When I grow up, I want to be a lot of things. I want to be an Interior Designer, while continuing to run and grow both my consulting business JUnique and all-natural bracelet company Kuponya…. I want to be Successful! But my dreams for the future are to be happy, healthy, and wealthy. I know that may sound like a simple life, but in those three things so much comes from it. In that future I want to change the world by impacting it in a positive way and leave a legacy to carry that on! I feel like nowadays with technology we are all distracted by the negative things and impressed with anything, and I want to set the bar higher on things that people are impressed and motivated by in life.

Although many girls have specific people, they admire I don't. I admire anyone who lives the way I aspire to live. Wealthy not rich, down to earth, and impactful in their community. But I do have a hero, and although it may sound cliché my hero is my dad! If not for him, I wouldn't even be writing this right now. I wouldn't have events, business ideas, speaking engagements; I wouldn't be an entrepreneur if it weren't for him! I may get in my teenage moods and not want to do anything but lay around, but he still motivates me to create, learn, and motivate other, and for that he is my hero.

To me an awesome girl is someone who knows their strengths and uses them to live their best life, while knowing their flaws and weaknesses and combining the two to make a difference in the world, and although I haven't mastered this equation just yet, I also think being an awesome girl is just being a positive girl in this world with hopes and dreams, and I am definitely that!

Affirmations

1. It's not new it's just you.

2. I'm worth my success.

3. Whatever I dream, I can achieve.

4. I make a difference.

5. Don't tell people your plans, show them your results.

Bio

Jayel Priester is truly the life of the party. At the age of four she was diagnosed with type one diabetes and because of this condition had to do things a little different from kids her age. Instead of looking at the negatives caused by her condition she decided to focus on the positives and embrace the she wasn't a "normal" kid. Her positive energy and outgoing personality have opened several opportunities for her. In elementary school she was a part of the daily school news program. In middle school she served on student council and in high school was a cheerleader. Jayel is always trying to find ways to challenge herself to do new things. In 2016 she did 30 minutes of yoga every day for the whole year. In 2015 Jayel started her first business, Kuponya, where she hand makes custom bracelets. Part of Jayel's mission is to encourage young people to embrace their uniqueness and know that it's OK to be different.

CHAPTER 19

ANTONIA WILLIAMS

Age: 18

Why Am I An Awesome Girl

An awesome girl is one that is a high achiever, one who strives for excellence, one who never gives up no matter what, one who goes after their dreams, and one who is beautifully and wonderfully made. With that being said, that is why I believe I am an Awesome girl. I am an Awesome Girl because I seek to inspire and give others hope and inspiration not only through my writing but through my speaking. I am an Awesome girl because I know my 'WHY' which helped me discover my passion. For my passion lead me to who I do it for and why I do it. I am focused and determined, and most importantly I do my best to stay consistent with working hard. Being an Awesome girl means being benevolent, uplifting, vibrant, elegant, admirable and so much more. The main thing to being an Awesome girl is always being there for other Awesome girls. I love to encourage and support other girls who are being awesome in their own unique way. I am an Awesome girl, because of the heart that I have. If your heart isn't right, then nothing else will be. You have to have heart to do the awesome things that you do. You have to have heart to love, and to share with the world how awesome of a girl you are. That right there is why I am an Awesome girl, because heart beats all those achievements and rewards if you don't truly have the love for doing it. I don't want to just stop at being awesome. I want to go even higher and level up even more, because being an Awesome girl is just where it all starts.

Affirmations

1. I am the architect of my life; I build its foundation and choose its contents.

2. My ability to conquer my challenges is limitless; my potential to succeed is infinite.

3. I acknowledge my own self-worth; my confidence is soaring.

4. I wake up today with strength in my heart and clarity in my mind.

5. I have the power to create change.

Bio

Antonia Williams is a 2x published Author and Spoken Word Artist. She wrote her first book at 15 years old titled 'Answers from God' and her second book a year later titled 'Call on Me'. She won 1st place at her first speaking competition at the SCLC youth oratorical contest. Since then she has continued to win 1st place at other various competitions and continues to strive for excellence with through her speaking and writing. She is a recent graduate of DM Therrell HS and will further pursue her career by joining the Army and going to college to major in communications.

CHAPTER 20

ANGELICA BLACKWELL

Age: 12

Why Am I An Awesome Girl?

The reason I am an awesome girl is because I can be myself and express what I love. I am independent and can do things on my own, like ride a bike. I am also kind: I treat everyone with kindness as I want them to do for me.

When I grow up, I would like to be an architect, and design and build houses for people who need it. My

67

goal is to make it so nobody will have to live on the streets. I really want to end poverty. So many people have to live off trash instead of real food. It makes me sad to see all the homeless people in the world. But when I am sad, I lift my spirits by drawing and listening to music. I really like to draw anime and listen to BTS, Twice or Dreamcatcher's. I like K-pop bands because I like to learn about different cultures, and one of the best ways to do that is through music.

I really admire Oprah Winfrey. Nothing came easy to her and she achieved success despite all the things that happened to her. Oprah had to build her way to fame from the ground up. But my heroes are my parents because they teach me so much about how to live my life. They taught me how to walk and how to talk. And my parents encourage me to dream. If I could invent one thing to make life better for someone else, I would make a fully automated wheelchair that operated on a remote control.

I really love being a girl. I like dressing up in pearl and lace dresses, I like having short hair or long hair and being able to flip it no matter what. I love my voice (but I hope it gets deeper as I get older!). I love being me. And I really hope other girls love being themselves, too. We are all awesome!

If you ever forget how great you are, say these affirmations:

Affirmations

1. You are Awesome.

2. You are Kind.

3. You are Smart.

4. You are Worthy.

5. You are Amazing.

Bio

Angelica Blackwell is a seventh grader at Simmons Middle School. She is an artist with a passion for manga and anime, loves K-pop bands, and her favorite book and movie is "Harry Potter: Chamber of Secrets". Although Angelica loves the water, she does not swim. She aspires to join the US Armed Forces upon graduation.

CHAPTER 21

TALECIA CLARK

Age: 16

Why Am I An Awesome Girl?

What makes me an awesome girl is that God created me different and special in my own way. I describe myself as strong and powerful because I am able to do things that are not required or easy for me to do and still succeed.

When I grow up, I want to be a pediatrician or a radiologist. I enjoy helping people and making them feel better. One thing I enjoy doing the most is cheering. I enjoy cheering people on to do

71

their best. I love learning new things while cheering and tumbling. There is always a new skill to learn. One person I look up to is my cheer coach Maci. Despite her illness, she is an awesome cheerleader and coach. She even does tucks with us at practice sometimes and she is a grown woman!

My hero is my mother. She helps me get through things that nobody else does. My dreams for the future are to grow up, be successful and accomplish my all dreams. One thing I would do to change the world is to take all of the violence out of the world and make it a safer place.

If I had to invent something it would be social media that does not require internet. Sometimes when you are in a place with poor internet connection it can get a little irritating because it either works slow or not at all.

What do I like about being a girl? I enjoy getting glammed up. Last year for my birthday, we went to the Beyoncé concert right after my cheerleading practice. We didn't have time for me to do my makeup and then my hair, so my friend Ryann did my makeup and my friend Makenzie did my hair. I really enjoyed it.

Bio

Talecia Clark attends Hueytown High School and plans to attend Emory University in Atlanta. She aspires to be a Physical Therapist or a Radiologist. Talecia enjoys cheerleading and tumbling, her favorite book is *Letters From Rifka*, and she very creative.

CHAPTER 22

MIRANDA GREENE

Age: 18

Why Am I An Awesome Girl?

I like being a girl because I know that the power that I have is automatically underestimated by anyone else that does not possess it. I know that I have the creativity to be an artist, the strength to be a lawyer, the patience to be a doctor, and the passion to be whatever else that was not specifically created for me. In society, we are taught that women are to be strong, but not stronger than the man, or else the man will feel intimidated. I feel as though intimidation is a good thing. Intimidation works in favor of those who are often underestimated. And the most underestimated being on earth is the woman.

I am an Awesome Girl because I know that I am strong. I know that when I am going through something and the smoke clears and it is just me and everyone else has gone back to their own lives, I am the one who pulls myself out of the hole that I have sunk myself into. I am an Awesome Girl because I know that I am stronger than the heartbreak, the gossip, the failing, the loss. I am an Awesome Girl because even if these trials were designed to break me, I know that I was crafted to where instead, they will shape me.

I would describe myself as loyal. I am loyal to those who even have failed to return the favor, but I know that if I lowered myself to their level, I would no longer be loyal to myself. I have vowed to myself to never let the shortcomings of other people change or diminish my own morals and values. I am a forgiving person. Forgiveness is necessary for personal growth, and to forgive does not mean to forget. I am a loving person. Unconditionally. The only hatred in my heart is for actions, never for the person.

I admire all of the women who are real. The women who make a name for themselves, despite the popularity of their spouses, siblings, or parents. I admire all of the women who do not put down other women, in hopes of receiving praise from men. I respect all of the women who embrace the positive and negative stereotypes centered around us. Femininity is not a flaw. It is a strength that only we possess. No matter how much it is tried to be dimmed, eliminated, or criticized, it cannot be taken away.

Affirmations

1. I strive to demand what I want to receive, instead of accepting what I am given.

2. I am bigger than my situation.

3. I am only responsible for my own shortcomings, not others'.

4. I am better than the pain that I may feel.

5. I have the ability to overcome any obstacle.

<u>Bio</u>

Miranda Greene is a freshman at the University of Montevallo. She aspires to be a successful published author and owner of an organization that provides books to emerging nations to combat illiteracy. Miranda enjoys reading, styling fashion "looks", watching YouTube videos, and resting. Her favorite books are "A Thousand Splendid Suns" and "The Hate U Give". Miranda also loves foreign languages: "I know enough of Spanish and French to hold a conversation in both languages."

CHAPTER 23

TE'AIRA HEGGLER

Age: 16

Why Am I An Awesome Girl?

Do you want to know why I believe I am an awesome Girl? I believe I am awesome girl because I was selected to attend Ramsay High School, which is an alternative school, which not many students are accepted into this school. I was a cheerleader for my middle school, and I really enjoyed it. I am also a member of Saint Paul A.M.E. Church and I am on the usher board.

I would describe myself as is

pretty, smart, funny, caring, curious, and lovable. Each word is meaningful to me because I love when people call me pretty. When someone is down, I try to make a joke just to make them laugh. I am caring because I always care about people and I babysit my little cousin on the weekend. I am loveable because when it comes to my family, my church family, and my friends, I love them so much and they have a special place in my heart.

I like to read, and I like to play with my brothers and my baby cousin. My favorite thing to do is help my momma and grandma around the house. I admire my mom because she is a great mom and she is smart and pretty. When I grow up, I would like to follow in my mom's footsteps. She is my hero because she sacrifices her time for her friends even if she has a lot to do that day. My mom will love on you no matter what, even if I make her mad still will say, "I love you TT." She is the most selfless person I know besides my grandma.

My grandma always put her family and friends first no matter what. Whenever I'm hungry my mom always asks, what do you want me to cook for you" and I love her for that. Whatever I tell my mom her response is, "I understand TT," even though she is probably tired of me. I love my mom with all my heart, and I couldn't have asked for a better mom. That is why my mom is my hero.

My dreams for the future are to graduate from high school and college, become a teacher and mortician, and be a successful woman in life. I will work to stop gun violence because there are so many families hurt because they have lost a love one in their family, including mine when my brother died. I also say killing people is not the answer because when you kill someone you don't know who you are hurting. If I could, I would invent a love machine so we can learn how to love one another.

The thing I like about being a girl are that I get to dress nice, get my hair done, and when I want to say hello to another girl, I just say it - we don't have to punch each other's arms to say hello like boys.

Words that I have and want to give to young beautiful ladies out there in the world are

1. You can be whatever you want in life.
2. Don't let anyone discourage you from doing that.
3. Always follow your dream and DREAM BIG.

Teaira Heggler is a student at Ramsay High School who aspires to obtain her degree in education to become a teacher. She also plans to become a mortician. In her spare time, Teaira enjoys babysitting her cousins. She doesn't have a favorite book because "I like them all!" Teaira loves sports, especially football.

CHAPTER 24

ELISA CHRISTINE SAFFOLD

Age: 16

Why Am I An Awesome Girl?

The question is why I believe that I am an awesome girl. If you're looking for my answer to be just simply broad, then you should stop reading now. The answer to that question goes far beyond simple characteristics such as: cute, funny, loving, and caring. There is never a simplistic answer when you ask a young woman about who she is. Diving deeper into who I am inside and out will give you a different insight on how young women as myself view themselves when they look in the mirror daily.

What makes me an awesome girl is my undesirable passion for helping others before myself, my positive and encouraging attitude in everything I do, and my to-die-for smile that I always show to make other's day. I believe I would describe my overall personality as compassionate and benevolent. Even on my worst days, I do not hesitate to help others who are in need, even if it means giving them my last dime. Every day I think about individuals who are not as fortunate as me and if I were in their shoes, I would desire for someone to help me. The attitude that I carry with me every day is always joyous because I believe in being the light everywhere, I go. When others see the beautiful smile, I show on my face, it makes them smile and if they are feeling down my smile allows them to realize that trouble does not last always and there is always a better day coming. I think the idea of how I see myself physically on the outside goes hand in hand with being an awesome girl.

When I think about the question, "What do you want to be when you are older?", I think passed just a career; the question that comes to mind is, "When I am older, who do I truly desire to be as an individual and what do I want to be doing to help develop myself and others?". My answer is, when I grow up, I do not desire to be famous, I simply desire to be known within communities as someone who gives back to those who live without the necessities to make a living every day. In my eyes, it is always the little things that makes a big difference. As far as a career goes, I would like to be a homicide detective. I chose this career because discovering the individuals who have done faulty deeds makes me believe I am doing something productive and helpful. Giving families the necessary reassurance about me finding who might have taken their loved one's life is heartwarming and then actually finding the bad guy is even more exciting. My mentality towards helping others in my opinion makes me an awesome girl.

Bio

Elisa Christine Saffold is a junior at Ramsay High School. She is a member of the basketball team, aspires to attend college on basketball scholarship, and attain her degree in Criminal Justice. Elisa then plans to serve in the military and become an agent with the Federal Bureau of Investigation.

Regina Sunshine's
Awesome Girl Affirmation
I Was Born to Win!

I was born to win.

I am more than a conqueror.

I was created for greatness.

I was born to be victorious.

I will achieve my dreams.

I can be anything I choose.

I can do anything I set my mind to.

I am a champion.

I am worthy of the best things in life.

I am worthy of the dreams in my heart.

I am worthy of living a great life.

I am an Awesome Girl.

A Letter from Regina to You, Awesome Girl!

From My Heart to Yours,

I hope you were blessed by the stories on these pages and saw yourself in the lives of our Awesome Girls. I hope that you think about all of the things that make you an Awesome Girl and never allow anyone to convince you that you aren't. Learn to love yourself and all the things that are special about you. And when you are ready, use these next pages to write your own chapter and let's continue this journey together to inspire, motivate and empowerment the next generation of Awesome Girls.

Be Blessed. Keep Winning!

Regina Sunshine

Author: _____

Age: _____

Why Am I An Awesome Girl:

_____
_____
_____
_____
_____
_____
_____
_____
_____
_____
_____
_____
_____
_____
_____
_____
_____
_____
_____
_____
_____
_____
_____
_____
_____
_____

Affirmations

1. _____

_____

2. _____

_____

3. _____

_____

4. _____

_____

5. _____

_____

ABOUT THE CURATOR

Regina Sunshine Robinson is an Author, Motivational Speaker, Talk Show Host, Empowerment Coach, Corporate Trainer, and Teacher. She is the CEO of the Regina Sunshine Global Network, parent company to everything Regina Sunshine including EWATE, a Women's Empowerment Organization whose main purpose is to empower and encourage women to be all they were created to be in order to fulfill God's perfect plan for their lives. Regina's personal motto is "It's Not Over Til I Win" and she wins when she sees others "WINNING". For more information, go to ReginaSunshine.com.

www.ingramcontent.com/pod-product-compliance
Lightning Source LLC
LaVergne TN
LVHW041232080426
835508LV00011B/1175